Clydebuilt

Clydebuilt

Owen Gallagher

Smoke Stack Books

Smokestack Books
1 Lake Terrace, Grewelthorpe, Ripon HG4 3BU
e-mail: info@smokestack-books.co.uk
www.smokestack-books.co.uk

ISBN 9781916012165

Smokestack Books
is represented
by Inpress Ltd

for
Ruth, Jessie,
Rory, Jaida
and Regan

Contents

Soot

Each time I flick a light switch
I see mother strapped to a chair.

A white-coated man throws a lever.
Her body thrashes like a live cable.

I nurse my heart with its image
of mother framed in the doorway,

dressed as if in mourning,
her temples blackened

from repeated shocks.
I nurse my heart for the mother

who never came back.
She lived in a darkness

no prescription could lift.
I am the soot from her chimney.

Fathering Mother

She went from tenement to tenement,
wore a full apron beneath her coat,
carried a stiff-wired brush and a metal pail.

She was one of Ireland's lost daughters,
I, all clothes on bones, too young
to be schooled, parked on each flat's

outside stairs while she swept, scrubbed
till their stone was clean as our own.
Her hair was bramble and fiery red, her face

a pool of freckles. She dipped her brush in
and out of what she called 'the font',
and sang Lovely Leitrim, a comforter,

in those acres of cold concrete,
that took her back into the flower-banked lanes
of Ballinamore, leading cows to byres.

Once, I found mother on our own stairs,
tears pumping out of her. My tiny hands gloved hers.
I was her father, her son, her skin, her tears.

The Terrible Twins

Though drawn from an Irish womb
I was delivered in another country.

'C is for?' mother asked as I learned
the name of each Irish county by heart.

Ireland was a jigsaw. All of the counties
locked perfectly into their neighbours,

each with a tiny capital. After I'd snapped
Wexford onto Wicklow, Meath onto

Monaghan, I sped northwards into Armagh
and Antrim. There were no visible

differences between these border counties
in 'The North' and those in 'The South'.

'The terrible twins' mother called them.
Ireland was a jigsaw I could assemble

in the dark, the shape of an ear, the top
right corner bitten off, a dog in a fight.

Newspapir Boy Meets Goliath

Ah strode intae an early wurld stalked by a giant
an witnessed a man dreep doon a drainpipe,
pub doors openin tae knocks like thi Morse Code,
an a queue already formed ootside the pawn shop;

Father Chalmers sprintid wi rosary beads in haun,
Uncle Hugh bolted frae a tenement,
shirt-tail flappin, my father stood on a street corner
hopin tae be chosen fir wurk.

The giant boy trailed me intae a close
tae theive ma paper-round,
snatched ma satchel an ma list, placed a finger
oan his lips then droo it across his throat.

Ah walked aff like that yung fella in the Bible,
intae the Valley of Elah, plucked a marble frae
ma pockit, turned an raised ma sling.

Cat-flap wi Bells

It wisnae thi street vendir's
black cat costume,
nor hur spiel thit collared mi
intae signin' a direct debit
fir thi Cat Protection League.

It wis thi bag ah kittens
muthir hid thrust intae ma hawn,
thit meowed awe thi way
tae Glesca Bridge.

Aged seven, ah stood, legs braced,
throo thi bag er thi parapet
an' watched it sink,
pop up an bob
in ma heid ever since.

Hence thi direct debit,
thi cat-flap, fish heids,
saucers ah milk,
thi wind-up-mouse.

Cut!

For fifty years you've censored
this film. Don't leave.
You're almost through.

Spool back to the opening scene
where you enter the toilet
and the man follows you in.

Listen to the screams
of the kids in the cinema
as you stand at the urinal,

your heartbanging
like a clapperboard.
What's the man saying?

Don't edit the script.
Release this footage.
Focus. Flick forward.

You told the ice-cream man
you were sore when he found
you in the cubicle.

Don't stand off-screen.
You have the lead part
in a cast of two.

A Very Private Crucifixion

I want Mr Johnston stripped,
nailed to the page,
crucified with every word,
the way he had me stripped, limbs pinned by my classmates
against the blackboard.
His eyes focussed
on my
thirteen-year-old body,
head bowed,
body drained
like Jesus
on the cross
on the wall above my head.
When the lookouts crowed,
he would click
his fingers
three times.
I would dress,
slump at my desk,
and write:
'I must not tell!'
'I must not tell!'
'I must not tell!'

Kissin' thi Corpse

Thi first corpse ah kissed
wis Pat McGinnis,
a Clare man fae Ennis,
who lodged in Glescae wi' Aunt Alice.

'Never afore hid this bachelor
bin kissed sae much, if ever,'
said muther, as she hauled me ower
Pat's coffin.

Tho ah went oan tae kiss less o' thi deid
than thi livin', ah hae often dwelt
on how mony hae wept,
'n' wished:

Oh, tae bi kissed, wance, 'n' kissed
as if I'll bi missed.

Crawlin' 'n' Trawlin'

Afore Sunday mass ma da wid balance mi
oan his knee, trawl ma scalp wi' a metal comb

tae see if lice hid dared tae land, sabre thaim
wi' a thumbnail, an' flush thi corpses doon thi sink.

(At times hail continents o' lice wur on thi move,
driftin' snowfields that turned intae an avalanche

when ah sneezed. Ah watched is thay landed
ontae ma mates heids – their ma's demanded

ma exclusion frae skool).When ma scalp wis free
frae these bloodsuckers ma da wid massage

Fairy Soap thro ma hair, lea it tae set
in wave efter wave:

a frozen ocean nae heid lice cood scale;
a rock face nae fitba cood dent.

Carbolic

I ordered it online. A short trawl, click and send.
Couldn't resist the sweet tarry smell that soaped me
from the tin-bath to the public baths; the vapour of coal

tar and pine squeezed into soap doorstops, mined
from forests toppled by the cold.
There was no gel, no Head 'n' Shoulders then, only

a chunk of 'orange or green?' sold by the ounce or pound,
cut like a slice of cheddar from a massive
round on a counter to zap creepy crawlies

partying on scalps, and soothe ferocious bites
from creatures in the mattress with alligator mouths.
Bodily odours were masked with a fragrance

that filled classrooms and wards and sedated rowdy elements
on dance floors. Women kept chunks in handbags
as a cosh in self-defence or as a deodorant, midges

when they got a whiff passed out in droves.
Mothers used the soap like smelling salts
to hoist husbands back to a level of consciousness

after a night of 'goldies' and to wash the mouths
of children who swore. It was stacked like the pyramids
of Egypt in public baths, kept the Empire clean,

and has resurfaced in its original form
beside basins in our cities and in Red Cross areas
overseas. I wait for the letterbox to clatter
to unwrap and lather the past, disinfect what is not seen.

I Could Have Been a Legend

When I read that Roy Rogers had galloped into Glasgow
and then hit the trail without my knowing, I ripped out
the front page picture of some snotty-nosed greenhorn
shaking Roy's hand, and riddled it with bullet holes.

Roy'd been streets away while I rode through alleys
in my home-made cowboy duds reducing the city's
crime rate and putting more bodies
in Boot Hill than Billy the Kid.

Policeman Pat Garrett always tipped his hat at me.
If Roy'd seen the prizes I'd won at fairground rifle ranges,
and watched me lasso a lollipop from a kid's mouth,
he would've pleaded for me to be his sidekick.

He'd have envied my bullet-proof vest of comics,
and Trigger would have dipped his head when I sang,
'A four legged friend...' I could've been Roy's stand-in!
But mother never leaked he was in town.

She knew he'd rope me off to a Hollywood set,
that I'd marry a 'Queen of the West',
serenade her with 'My Chickashay Gal',
whistle for Trigger and Bullet at dawn.

Lavender

On those rare Saturdays father was at home
the whole house breathed of lavender
as if he'd just picked the purple flower domes
and crushed them into the canister
while on his knees in the hallway,
slabbing chunks of polish
on the linoleum, working his way
back, he'd buff till it shone like varnish
which was my cue to skate in socks,
across the hall, knowing we were in sync
and he'd catch me in the lock
of his arms, a silent clunk, click, and wink.

The Cold War

Desperate to ditch short trousers and chuck my glasses
I became Secret Agent 008. My mission?
To undermine parental control.

I appointed myself Minister of State for Children,
recruited cousins and friends, scheduled
training for sleepers and informants.

I held passing-out ceremonies in the Goldenshed,
pinned milk bottle tops on those who went
beyond the call of duty.

Parents cruel as Stalin were tailed, aunts who silenced
a house with a look and uncles who broke into
piggy-banks were logged.

We drilled peep-holes and took fingerprints,
ordered duplicate keys, learned Russian,
Mandarin, Irish.

Until my body was stretched suddenly
in every direction. Fields of hair
appeared overnight.

My testosterone levels exceeded all known
medical records. Renting my brother's
long trousers, I assigned myself a different mission.

Plectrum

Accordin' tae muther, thi three brass baws
wir thi Faither, Son, 'n' Holy Ghost.
Pray hard enough, she declared, *an' we shall receive.*

Each Monday, afore evenin' mass, ah'd lay
hur offerings oot oan thi pawnbroker's altar.
Each Friday he askd whit ah'd cum tae redeem.

Ah yearned fur thi guitar muther hud asked mi tae pawn;
tae pluck its strings, skite mah fingers
across thi fret boord till thay stung;

an' prance aboot at an assembly oan thi skool stage.
Nae amount o' praying moved thi patron saint
o'music tae intervene.

Wan cloudy nicht ah stood aw in black
wi a glass-cutter in haun.

The Austerity Pizza

Your deep-fried pizza, priced at a fiver,
    scooped from the pool of the fish-fryer

was a cratered disc of crusty batter
    topped with Ketchup and dollops of Tartare.

We biked it home for your birthday supper.
    The pizza cooled in the cardboard carrier.

The lift yanked and clanked us higher
    and higher up the dodgy tower.

Your mother seized a pizza slicer,
    cut enough portions for a class of toddlers;

a ruse to convince your younger sisters
    they'd be so full they wouldn't want afters:

a squirt of cream on a King-size Mars Bar
    and Irn-Bru distilled from rusty girders.

For Your Penance Say Ten Decades of the Rosary

Some penitents feared voice recognition, attended churches
elsewhere. Most were like sprinters, in and out
of the confessional box before you could finish a Hail Mary.

Youngsters like me eavesdropped, failed to comprehend;
'And did you come, my child?' 'And did you do in return?'
There was comfort in this act of revelation, being cleansed

weekly from the grime of sin. I walked away light-headed
determined not to steal my neighbour's pen or covet his bike.
Confession was the Marmite which gelled church and church-goer.

Sins decomposed as you rose from your knees and you felt
you could get ten out of ten for spelling and just might
be chosen for the school football team. As a reserve.

Amen

It was the mystery of it all:
the huge oak doors I would push,
the echo it made when I stepped inside
the great cavernous house,
familiar as home, glass, timber, stone,
filled with statues, pews and fonts,
the scent of lilies that reminded me
of when the dead were buried,
mostly on Saturdays, a smell that greeted me
as I would genuflect,
enter the sacristy, don the black robe,
the white surplice.

It was all a mystery, a kneeling place for faith
to light its candle,
where pledges were made from the kingdom
of words and neighbours
would queue on Fridays to confess a well of sin,
mend their souls,
stand like a lighthouse in the family again.

But it was the mystery of Latin I thirsted for most,
the tabernacle of language:
Confíteor Deo omnipoténti, beátæ Maríæ
semper Vírgini,
beáto Michaéli Archángelo, beáto Ioanni Baptístæ,
sanctis Apóstolis
Petro et Paulo, ómnibus Sanctis, et vobis…

The rising and falling of its oars,
where my tongue longed to row,
the learning of it by heart,
a boat pushed out daily
to early and evening mass,
the dark chocolaty flavours
that never melted in the mouth,
an ancient recipe that bound me
and that I still recite
to savour the sounds.

The Whisky Fairy

Our tenement was crammed with connoisseurs
of Scotch Whisky who could tell an Aberfeldy malt

from a Ye Monk's blended. 'Masters of the Nose'
we called them, their nozzles purple and pocked.

Blindfolded tastings were followed by a liquid history
of a given brand. These old fellows had the mind

of a Whiskypedia. They were the Keepers of the Quaich.
Once a month, before milk floats tinkled, a bottle

of the 'water of life' appeared on our doorsteps,
a gift from the 'Whisky Fairy' who'd kept us awake

by hammering and chiselling an entrance through
the gable wall of the Whisky Bond in our back court

to fetch the 'liquid gold'. The bricks were replaced
and repointed before the first shift clocked in.

I raise a glass each night to toast the farmers
for harvesting the grain, the brewers who performed

a miracle, the coopers for the casks they made,
and that 'Whisky Fairy' who can never be named.

Thi Clyde Runs Thru Mi

Ah wis reared in a toon whaur alsations guarded milkmen,
gas meters wur robbed mid-week
'n' conductors rarely asked
fur fares oan thi lest bus hame.

Where it paid tae bi alert iz a commando
parachuting intae enemy territory,
and wiz safer tae lea thro back courts,
scale walls lik' spiderman,
an' skite doon telegraph poles intae alleyways

than bi challenged bi youths oan thi street
in a scene thit cood've bin shot in 'High Noon'
whaur thae droo nae guns but razors
and snarled; 'Celtic or Rangers'?
which prompted a startin' pistol
tae gae aff in ma heid.

There wis nae careers advice
tae show how thi future micht blow.
Tae escape ye hud tae outwit yer opponents
oan thi field wi' a baw, or don a dog-collar.

The Lone Red Guard of the Clydeside

Smart in a denim cap and tunic, I marched out
of my tenement, a Red Guard clutching

Mao's book in its soft vinyl cover, chanting,
'Long live the proletariat!' to the road sweeper,

bus conductor, mothers pushing prams, and quoted
passages from *Contradictions Among the People*

in bars to friends when they didn't put up a round,
to club bouncers for manhandling the masses,

and sat in Chinese restaurants with my red book
on the plate, ready at the snap of a cracker

to down chopsticks and lecture the waiters
on revolutionary thought. Eager to empower

the working class I read aloud in the factory
canteen to suddenly vacated seats, took pride

in threats from management, and dreamt of advising
Comrade Mao on the West's imperial dogs.

When my great leader passed away,
'The Little Red Book' fell from its pedestal.

I donned a beret, and smoked a cigar, studied
Guerrilla Warfare.

Where Trees Didn't Leaf

South Side Sawmills, Glasgow

Sawdust fell when passers-by shook their heads,
dossers scooped it up to skin with tobacco,
birds dived, and soared with curly shavings.

Hardwood and softwood trunks, from Borneo
to Brazil, shipped to the sawmills, were laid out
like handmade cigars and left to season in yards

for cladding, clothes pegs and coffins. Workers
debated the origins of trees by smell and touch,
feared fingers sawn off, backs snapped.

I swept up sacks of sawdust, heaved them onto
trucks to line the nation's pet cages, and for barmen
and school janitors to scatter over vomit.

The old hands told stories of gangsters driven here
by rivals at night, reduced to slices of meat sold
from a dodgy butcher's van. I eased my nerves

with Bounty bars longing for the whining
and grinding of saws to cease as I stepped between
creaking log piles dreading the scream: 'Timber!'

The Field Recording Sessions

A tape deck stowed beneath my bed, I'd press
Record when Brigid, Kathleen, or Tess,
turned their back to undress.

My flat-mates ears were pressed
to the door as I, in a Che Guevera vest,
put my seductive talents to the test.

On the feast day of St.Agnes,
a taxi load of mothers, on their holy quest,
believing we were possessed,
stormed in with Father Rowan to wrest
us from the Devil's breast.

Holy water doused the mattress
to exorcise the voice of Tess,
from the deck beneath the bed, 'Yes! Yeeesss!'

Ir Yoo Lookin' it Me Jimmy?

Sumo barrels o' flesh dressed lik' best men
wir hired as bouncers in dance clubs,

yet whin Slasher or Scalper swaggered in
wi thair entourage o' rising stars

they wurni frisked fur nails ur razors
ur asked fur an admittance fee

as hauns* clapped doon clubbers lik' us.
Handbags wur stuffed wi' ower-proofed spirits

nae boozer wid stock, 'n' steel combs
thit cuid furrow a face.

Ir yoo lookin' it me Jimmy?
brot polis vans 'n' ambulances.

Wallflowers lik' me wur escorted ontae thi flair
bi thorny roses, snogged 'n' groped,

trotted aff tae a close tae perform acts
ah cannae disclose.

Claes-horses

Whitever thi waither, thi three o' us, kitted out
like Columbo, pulled oan unlit cigars.

We deserved Emmy awards fur delivering his line:
'Where did yi git thae shoes?'

tae security warkers 'n' shop-assistants
while we nicked thi latest Levis, 'n' Byfords.

Oor coats hud mair pockets than Fagin's.
Oor hauns wur quicker than a shirt-maker's

in a sweatshop. Windae dressers wondered;
'Did ah nae dress that mannequin?'

We strutted wi' Seturday nicht fever oan thi toon
boardwalks in oor latest collections,

left thi dance flair huvin swiped bras as souveniers,
hummin' Columbo's signature tune.

Guinness Black

Spare mi
thi endless elbowing
in high streets,
queuing
fur a changin' room,
slippin' oot o'
an' intae endless suits
o' colours 'n' cuts,
straight legs ur turn-ups,
double-breested ur vented,
considerin' lapels
narrow iz a hem,
wide iz a sleeve,
mutterin', 'it'll dae'
only tae queue in 'Returns'
an' despite statutory rights
bi refused a refund.

Naw!
Tailor mi
intae a handmade,
slimline suit
in Guinness black
thit offers a savvy
weekend supplement look
thit leads tae catwalks,
an' bein' clocked
by wumen who stop and gawp
plead fur a date, a snog,
who wolf-whistle
an' swoon
an' ah resuscitate
mooth tae mooth
an' ahm treatid rightly
iz a God.

Thi Gorbals Knot

A'richt,
ahm a fan o' thi tie.
No thi clip-on
ur pre-tied
school type,
thi keek at me!
kipper or Paisley patterned,
but thi skinny-malinky black,
beer 'n' slop resistant wan,
thit flags up
'style',
withoot stripes, ur hype.
Ah lik' thi way it pulls
mi together,
completes thi look,
gaes mi a rush,
a buzz, wi'oot thi use
o' powder, smoke ur drink,
undoes thi knot o' not
feelin' 'good enough',
allows mi tae whiz
thro closed doors
intae thi stores o' thi heart;
acts as a scarf, a bandage,
a sling fur a limb,
a substitute fur string
tae lower masel fae
a Juliet Balcony.

Sad

Sad was the father
who clutched his chest,
filled two sacks with medicines

and sat each night
in the dark
fearing the next attack.

Sad was the father
who couldn't say, 'I love you,'
before he dropped to the floor

and sad is the family choking
on words of love
still lodged in their throats.

McAlpine's Fusiliers

When father collapsed into his chair at night,
he stared into the fireplace of himself.
What stoked or doused his fire we rarely knew.
His tongue and hand were never raised at home.
The life went out of us when his heart gave in.

Our street was lined with hundreds of men
who stood awkwardly in suits. I half-
expected them to shoulder picks and shovels,
flank the hearse, and march like a regiment behind,
singing that Irish navvy song: *McAlpine's Fusiliers.*

An old ganger told me later that father could out-dig
any man and square a hole so plumb
it could be tested with a spirit level.
'He cemented every gang,' he said,
'and was always horsin' about.'

The old fella broke into song:
'As down the glen came McAlpine's men
with their shovels slung behind them,
'twas in the pub they drank their sub
and up in the spike you'll find them...'

Those who could sing, did,
and those like me who marveled at their camaraderie,
were angered that they were sweated to the bone
and their throats were caked with concrete
by the time they got home.

A Family Undertaking

It took a full day to build dad's coffin.
Mother mapped the outline of his only suit
onto a roll of woodchip wallpaper.

We each cut around a limb till we had a template,
laughed, bickered and cried as always,
while we sawed, glued and screwed offcuts

she bought from the sawmill.
Mother was the chief chippie. She took her lead
from a library book, issued orders

with the speed and force of a nail gun.
There was a queue at the wake. Kith and kin
marveled at the coffin; the headrest,

elbow wedges, the whole snug fit of it;
the smile chiseled on his face
we'd all had a hand in throughout the years.

I Watch My Dead Father's Shoes Being Taken

Glasgow, 1981

Those are my father's shoes on my uncle's feet,
the style like dad, plain and neat.

The leather, soft and tanned,
lined as the palm of my hand.

The heels steeled with a plate
to take dad's weight.

After years of 'polish 'n' shine',
I long to wear what's rightly mine.

'Wait,' Dad would say, so I will wait
and chalk my Uncle's life up on a slate.

Damned That He Was Irish

Damned that he was Irish, spoke Irish
and had rarely entered a school.

Damned when he was sold at a hiring fair
under De Valera's rule.

Damned that he made it to Glasgow
to be the butt-end of jokes.

Damned that all the years he navvied
he couldn't swell his pay poke.

Damned that he'd never donned the British
Army uniform to do his stint.

Damned that he sat with the Evening News
and couldn't unpick its print.

Damned for hardly speaking at home
and seldom turning on a light.

Damned that his pay was docked when he
had a stroke on the building site.

Damned that his heart gave up and he left
me as his namesake

and look-alike. Damned I am for having
never left his wake.

Sure I Hardly Knew You!

I never saw you laugh, father,
spin a story or crack a joke.
I never heard you sing, father,
or tap your foot to a note.
I rarely heard you speak, father,
the truth is, you barely spoke.

I never saw you dance, father,
whirl mother round the floor.
I hardly saw you, father,
you jumped to the ganger's roar.
I never heard, 'I love you!'
before you slumped behind the door.

Tea

When mother stopped off from cleaning houses,
I would have scrubbed and buffed ours heavenly bright
for her return. We would sit and slurp tea
and make the most outrageous noise.
each outdoing the other.
'I better be off,' she'd say, 'before I drop.'
She had floors to mop and windows
to clean before she could dream.

The day a policeman knocked on my door,
and muttered, 'Your mother's dead,'
and left, I sat and slurped my tea, recalling
how our cups rattled in their saucers from laughter,
how she winked as she rose, wiggled her nose.
I cleaned my house till it gleamed.

Keek

Too often ah keek intae thi past
'n' catch Sheila Brogan
squinchin back
frae hur tenement flat.

Whit if ah hid seized thi black
rope o' hur hair
an' clippitty-clopped
in mah tackity boots
oer hur windae ledge,
then padded barefoot
up thi column o' hur back?

Whit if this?
'n' W*hit if that?*
are darts that zippity-zap
frae thi blowpipe
o' tickity hearts.

Kowtow

When the cabinet minister was obliged to dismount
from his bike and charged the policeman
with being a 'Fucking pleb!'
I thought of mother.

After she stood in the rain to pump the tyres
of the young Edward Du Cann's bicycle
she sprinted to open the gates of his estate
hurdling over puddles on the way.

As his Lordship pedaled past
in his waterproof Mac
she curtsied and wiped the spray
of muck from her dress and face.

2012

Thi Unoffishal Toorist Guide Oootside Glesca Central

'Ah'll show yoo anuther Glesca, wan wi heid bangers
sportin chibs tae stick in ribs an folk who hiv woke
tae find thair milk n meter munny nicked.
Ir greetid everi Friday wi a q it thi door:
loan sharks, rent arrears men, priests an spivs.
Where stray gulls n cats ir scoffd like Mars Bars
n weans scalps hiv bin mauled by nits.
Don't bi connd bi cafs n galleries
there's sods here who wipe thair gobs wi fivers
n widnae think twice o payin someone's ma
wi lefters an claes unfit fir charity.
Folk here hiv nae mair holes in thair belts tae tighten
tae fit sum right hoorable's stratigy.
Firget thi toorist hype, 'Glesca's great!'
Ah'll tell yoo aboot thi Clydeside thit made thi English
Government pipe thit thi Revolooshun wid start here
n planked tanks n gangs o strike breakers.
Dae yi want a bleached version o Glesca?
Wan thit's bin writtin oot o thi history books?
Ah've git three weans tae feed. Ah'll dae it fir a cuple a quid!'

Counter-surveillance

The plain clothed police woman in this coffee bar
is taking notes, monitoring my friend,
a student, three tables away as he watches
a live demo on his laptop.

He talks like a driving instructor: 'Turn
Left. Right. Right again.'
He is steering protesters away
from where they could be kettled.

My friend has a Glaswegian accent,
thick as a Scotch pie.
He acts like a commander
in a police operations room

and by switching between live coverage
on SKY News and the BBC,
he leads the students
out of the Whitehall maze.

A collision occurs at the woman's table.
Her notebook has gone. She rises,
slumps as if hit by a baton.
My friend still offers instructions.

I stroll out, and scroll through her notes,
salute officers with shields and dogs,
wink and say, 'Evening all'.

The Home Secretary Addresses the Prime Minister

All is as we found it, Prime Minister:
the Red Box containing the Budget, his hip-flask
and phone; no good-bye letter; nothing sinister.
It's as if he'd been summoned to task

by the patron saint of tax collectors, St. Matthew.
The duty officer said he was in good spirits
when he entered Number 11. We will pursue
all leads. There have been no hits

on his bank accounts. We doubt he'll appear
for his Budget speech. Security is fully stretched.
With protesters outside Westminster we fear
for your safety. RAF Northolt is on full alert.

Cook insists before your TV appeal,
you've an egg with the British Lion seal.

The Accumulation of Capital

Marx and Engels drained this bar in Soho
when they downed the last words

of *The Manifesto of the Communist Party.*
Here, thirsting for another round,

I now consider pickpockets:
not the ones working streets and malls,

nor those in Parliament who'll reduce
the amount we spend at tills,

but this one, kitted out like a toff,
currently lifting my friend's wallet.

I ram behind his knees the full force of justice,
haul him to his feet, and lecture him,

mercilessly, on the nature of Capitalism,
how it encourages thieves.

Humankind

A bearded man in a shalwar kameez
boarded the Tube with his phone and rucksack;
panic travelled at the speed of the train.

Passengers pulled emergency handles
in their heads. Thumbs raced to text:
'I love you,' pictures were sent.

The doors opened. The carriage emptied
and filled up again. The man's head
kept nodding and his lips were moving.

Some said he was praying. Some who didn't
back away, recognised when he adjusted
his headphones: 'Born in the USA...'

The Karl Marx Appreciation Society

Comrades,

As secretary, I'm delighted to ask you to attend
Karl's birthday party on the 5th May.

Though increasingly stooped with personal debt
his mind and tongue are faster than Google.

The prescription for his lenses has multiplied
but that doesn't deter him from predicting the future.

He can hear the Dow Jones Index rise and fall
before the stock exchange opens. We are hosting

the celebration in the Lenin Room and request you
dress as a heroic figure of our revolutionary past.

For the best look-alike, Mrs Marx will present
the winner with a signed copy of Karl's Poems.

No doubt he'll request Pin the Tail on the Donkey
and Charades. A defibrillator will be on stand-by.

Comrade Einstein

RSVP: The Marx Memorial Library

The Flautist of Westminster

In the roof-top restaurant of the Houses of Parliament
a young woman pulled out a flute
and played Ravel's 'Bolero'.
MPs froze on bar-stools.

Cabinet Ministers' knives and forks were suspended
in mid-air. Members in the Commons,
the Prime Minister on his battlement,
were silenced.

The flautist piped them all down to the river
into the care of the Ferryman.
He counted them on board
and off again in Hell.

Rookie and Cadre

Will the socialist revolution
lead to the withering of the State?

What occurred in Russia? China?
How does Cuba rate?

And what is the role
of the working class?

I asked, as I topped up the vodka
in the cadre's glass.

She was passionate: *The workers*
are the Revolution's bulldozer.

I plotted to remove the barricade
beneath her pullover.

The Arms Trade

Hearing of a request for an instrument
of death they swoop onto our estate.
They have no website or business card

to sell rifles and guns from the boot
of a car alongside pit bulls guaranteed
to eat and excrete your enemies.

Knuckle-dusters and machetes are two for one.
Drop-dead poisons are on special –
bouncers and minders on speed-dial.

A sliding scale of rates range
from teeth extractions to assassinations –
backhanders to the boys in blue not included.

Police records can be erased,
new identities created with the assistance
of Her Majesty's employees.

Limb and corpse disposal is available
to Gold Card holders.
Late payments are taken in severed ears.

I Saw a New World Being Assembled

In the tenements
there were workers
who built dreams for others,

singers who got drunk
on rebel songs,
fighters who fought

for themselves
in the workplace
and lost every round

all in revolt against
an assembly line
of masters.

I saw a new world
being assembled
in a sweatshop

where dreamers,
singers, fighters,
unfurled a trade union flag,

their voices bolted
and welded into one.

The Blacklist

Everyone sped off at the end of their shift.
No one saw him sobbing in his car.
No one paused to say he deserved a star
for speaking out; that his courage was a gift.

He feared his wife's reaction to the news,
he'd been sacked instantly without pay,
and was on a blacklist for his views,
this was his last working day.

No one saw him reverse his car
into the river and drop out of sight.
His workmates sent a sympathy card.
His wife set his boss's car alight.

The Saddest Passing

in memory of Francis Fox, Ballinamore, Leitrim. 1875-1945

I can see the shaft of grandfather's cart piercing
his chest. Not in a field in Leitrim but in a street
in Glasgow. I can hear him gasp and grasp
the last of the strength he had as he stumbled
and crawled up the stairs of the tenement
to the flat where grandmother had laid the table
and with a last tap at the door, faint as his heart,
he fell back into fearing he would never again
lay eyes on his greatest love. The door opened
and when he saw her, he sighed and sank
into the light and felt his head being lifted
and placed in her lap and he smiled when
she rubbed his hand as if trying to bring him back.
And it was enough to be held and to go like that.

If He Was to Pass, Then So Would I

in memory of Margaret Fox, nee Gormley,
Ballinamore, Leitrim, 1880-1945.

And didn't grandmother hear and fear
a faint knock which drove her to leave
the table she had set for grandfather's dinner.
The fear crept through her, a small terror,
almost sucking the breath out of her.
And didn't her heart nearly give up
when she saw him clutching his chest
on the doorstep. Sensing he was about to go,
she lifted his head and holding his face
to her face, kissed him on the mouth
and eyes and cried. No kiss or hug
from her children could loosen the tug
she felt when he died and true to her word
didn't she she let go of earth's hold.

Christmas in Belfast

Before mass, the milk-runs, and paper-rounds,
she hauled her son in through the door,
(the soldiers had returned to barracks for a full belly).

Taking off her Sunday best, she laid him out
on the table to rest, scrubbed him clean,
and sewed him up where he peeped through.

And when she was done, his tie and suit pressed,
Pioneer Pin closing his breast, didn't she pour
paraffin over him, set him alight, so no one

could see what they'd done to her wee boy,
and didn't she go out into the street, kitchen knife
under her apron, and take three soldiers with it.

1991

Donegal

The sweet smell
of burning turf
as you pass through
the Rosses
Gweedore
and Cloughaneely
the sky as big
as a prairie
with bog roads
turf stacks
and a quietness
along the route
you'd swear
the county
had been abandoned
till sheep
force you to stop
and you hear
a whistle
and a dog
is doing its job.

The Road to Ireland

I would like to live in the West, at the edge
of the world, on a small-holding,
walk my cow each day to the milk shed
and see which hen I am beholden

to for laying the egg. I would change
wheat into loaves, fill my plate from the field,
stack turf like gold bars for the kitchen range,
and conceal my distillery in creels.

I would stand at the town's crossroads
and hear who's 'Wanted' across the border,
who is cavorting with who on the old bog roads
and who sprayed 'Ireland is out of order!'

The Shoe Last

It came with the old fellas' cottage: cast-iron, black
as an undertaker's shoes, three-pronged – a heel
and two soles to slap a boot onto.

I found no pin-hammer, glue or tacks, no boots either.
The house was cleared when they'd all passed.
Neighbours spoke of how sacks were used to sock feet

instead of boots which were often snatched from the dead
and caused family spats. I wondered if the three
bachelors who'd lived here had to share

a pair to stroll to Mass or saunter in to Oweny
McGeady's shop for a game of cards and took turns
to wear them to a wedding or a wake.

I use the last as a bookend to support Kavanagh,
Heaney, Boland, who bless the ordinary,
the likes of these old fellas – a toehold to the past.

Keeping the Tongue

Falcarragh Visitors Centre, Donegal

All evening I gave ear to men, women and children,
singing in Irish, *Sean-nós,* low, mournful,

as if at a graveside, fearing they might be overheard,
charged with sedition, slung into a cell in these converted

barracks, or onto a coffin ship. Each song a throwing
of earth on the dead. Something was being passed on,

someone quietly held to account. And there was I, who
had no Irish, recalling how this my parents' first tongue

had been outlawed, starved, evicted from its holding,
forced into exile, fit only for bog men and those for sale

at hiring fairs. I sat amongst kinfolk, listenening to them
sing, applauding that they kept their tongue going.

The Cloughaneely Cutlass

At the heel of Muckish Mountain,
a turf-cutter struck an oak chest
with his spade.

Consider this old fella
when he found doubloons,
maps, and a cutlass
sharp as a Gillette blade.

What a treasure this cutlass is,
he thought, as he sliced through
the turf bank, minded by
a sub-zero winter,
and empty grate.

The Peat Door

Take this gift, carved from peat,
to hang on your key-ring.

It opens onto bogland,
roofed in acres of light.

There is turf to build a shelter,
an everlasting fire, cotton to dream on.

The bog protects and preserves,
serves as a filter,

absorbs darkness
and fuels hope.

Fill your pockets with heather
for the lapels of strangers.

Fill your shoes with moss,
an insole for your journey.

Not Letting On

I should have caught on: the constant peeing,
the stains at his crotch,
the disposable nappies in the bin.

I should have caught on when I stood outside
his farm-house door,
and heard him pray, loud and beseeching

fast, as if the more prayers he offered,
the more likely he'd be saved.
We were close but not close enough.

He didn't let on he was dying.
I didn't let on I knew.

Bleaching the Headstone

for John Gallagher

You were hard at it, dabbing bleach on the headstone,
scrubbing and sponging the Devil's grime
till the stone gleamed like the day it was set.

Given my hand was steadier, I wielded a child's paintbrush
and a palette of black. The dead arose slowly
and surely from the grave;

Sarah, our grandmother, bent over, screaming
as she was about to deliver her last child
and her last breath.

Her husband, John, who became mother and father
to seven, dragging stones from fields
to sow seeds in their place.

Charles, the bachelor, who'd urged me, a city boy, to milk
the bull in the byre, and churn the cesspit
till it turned to butter.

Mary, his sister, born with a small hill on her back,
driven to an asylum at an early age
and only released to this grave.

Your hand raced North, South, East and West
to bless yourself when we had finished
bleaching and tidying the plot.

We were closer now, closer than we had been in years
as close as the hairs on the brush.

The Water Thief

That the locals favour wellingtons
throughout the year
shows there's no shortage of water.

Yet it's been leaked that a neighbour
parked his tractor,
with an empty tank on a trailer,

at my outside tap and syphoned
enough to empty the local reservoir.
Perhaps his thirst was greater

or was it to top up
the Tullaghabegley River
and coax the return of that old otter?

Perchance it was connected
to a letter
from the Department of Water?

The Short Cut

A single track for a horse and cart had been cut
out by Kit Ferry's ancestors between Boyle's
and her fields. She and her sons kept this path
to Falcarragh clear with spades and shears.

Its shoulder-high ditches were banked up
with moss-dressed boulders. Now, silver birches,
brambles and giant nettles have rooted,
allowing no two-footer right of way.

Birds, bees, and butterflies are neighbours
with hares, foxes and shrews in this century-old,
self-protecting, eco zone. The ghosts
of Kit and her brood go to and fro.

I, now keeper of her keys, stand unsure
whether to take the long route on foot or hire
a chainsaw and oust all that have settled here.

Away and Find a Bride!

Old Kit's stick was an extension of her arm,
cut from a silver birch. It propped up
her arthritic body and enabled her to shoo her three
bachelor sons out of the house to milk, plough and,
she prayed, sow words in the heart of a woman,
while she baked and, raked the fire, stoked up
hope that each would return with a sweetheart.

'Have you men no feelings between your legs?
Away and find a bride!' she'd yell. And off
they'd rush to Oweny McGeady's shop to play
dominoes and cards with the other single men.
These three are dead now, piled up in the same
grave, on top of Kit, who no doubt prods them
with her stick to get up and out.

Peat

She loves to get a whiff of burning peat
as we drive through Donegal
with the windows down.

As soon as we park at the cottage
she whips the tarpaulin off the stack,
and loads a basket with heavy, black, sods.

I snatch dry fuchsia twigs for kindling,
dress the grate, strike a match and watch
the flames torch the standing fuel.

All week we keep feeding the fire
till the whole house is doused with the smell,
then we inhale our fill

and stuff the car's boot with peat
for the sniff, the gift of it, at home.

Reilly's Bar, Darwin

When my pint was capped
with a creamy head
and the shape of a shamrock

I thought of the cream of Ireland
pouring from every county
and how I flinched at the airport

when mother's tears flooded
the Departure Lounge like those
of thousands of mothers before her

and father stood to one side
looking as if a hearse
had hauled his heart away.

Fish R4U

In 2011, the Catholic Bishops of England and Wales re-established the eating of fish on Fridays.

Perhaps the saint responsible for penances
won the toss with God: once again
worshippers can queue outside
Only Cod for the flesh of fish,
eased down with salt 'n' vinegar
and blessed at the family table with Ketchup.

I suspect the Bishops' earthly advisers
are unaware of increasingly fishless seas
and have not hooked up with the fish gods
in Brussels, captains in suits
determined to restock our waters,
who have prescribed laws like Moses,
sunk more boats than Drake,
and forced trawler-men to beach
their boats on e-bay.

Perhaps a miracle will occur and parishioners
will be able to queue on Fridays at church
to receive a sliver of fish.

I offer these thoughts in the name of the Cod,
the Plaice, and the Haddock.

Fearing the Wrath

When I discover this book on a hotel bedside table,
I am reminded of 'Rocky Raccoon', who
'checked into his room, only to find Gideon's Bible'.

I ring Reception if I am not greeted
by this comforter, with its blood-red colour
and the plea on its cover: 'KINDLY

LEAVE THIS BOOK IN VIEW, THE NEXT GUEST
MAY NEED IT.' Even for a hard-nosed atheist
these Boys' Own stories make good reading.

They often end up in a coat pocket, which might explain
why one point seven billion have been distributed
or perhaps God has withdrawn them for revision,

pending a new edition. I flick this one open to a dog-eared page;
'*And the graves were opened;*
and many bodies of the saints which slept arose,

and came out of the graves after his resurrection,
and went into the holy city,
and appeared unto many.'

Fearing I'll be greeted, when I wake for a piss,
by a roomful of zombies, I place it
in the drawer and drain the mini-bar.

I recall, as I leave, the scene in which Moses hurled
God's words at those who departed
from the heavenly road.

I place the book back on display, the plea on its cover
burning like a commandment.

We are Closing in Five Minutes

Leave me in a public library
with floor-to-ceiling wooden shelves,
rows and rows of little alleys

where I can wrestle with thinkers,
brush against painters,
and peel the skin from poems,

trek through the travel section,
or ski down slopes of the world wide web
to land amongst picture books

where I feel like Gulliver
as I step over tiny tots
who carpet the floor and yell

to their parents; 'Read it again! Once more!'
Where keyless kids sit alongside
those doing essays or a hundred lines,

or are too afraid to go home,
and those in search of a fix of print,
or a daytime abode.

I make for the 'New Arrivals,'
and place myself under house-arrest
until the librarian's voice booms.

The National Literacy Thief

Between lining-up and registration,
some picky little fingers slipped the glasses
from my jacket and left me blinded to print.

No doubt my spectacles will be auctioned
in the toilet to prevent me from elucidating
the curriculum, whilst I hunt through the Science Lab

and try to assemble an *ad hoc* pair
which will enable me to complete a roll call
and impart knowledge of subject and predicate.

Failing this I will offer the class Judas
an inducement to act as a guide dog
and lead me to the thief.

Red Snow

All he left was his brolly,
his briefcase
and that dismissal note.

No severance pay,
no letter propped
on the stove.

For thirty years
I was his hearth
and home!

I followed his footprints
across the fields,
perfect casts

of the man
I thought I knew.
His tracks stopped

at a level crossing.
The lines were still warm,
weeping snow.

The Talking Cure

Of all the couches in showrooms and flea markets,
this one should have been at auction. Instead,
it ended up in a skip on my estate.

It resembled that famous sofa where Freud's patients lay,
and where I intended to embark
on an odyssey of conversation with myself.

I shouldered it up three flights of stairs,
set it down in my bed-sit, and dressed it
with a Qashqai rug and Chenille cushions.

I set the alarm for a fifty-minute hour and stretched out
to take the consequences (the guilt, the rap, the loot),
and yapped until my session was up.

Slumped into a green tub chair with a cigar I concluded,
this patient should not despair
but is in need of more specialised care.

Before I Make My Ascension to Heaven

I want to be rigged up in a Harley Davidson wheelchair
and cared for by a Miss World Nurse, steered
to Big Sadie's to have my body tattooed with I LOVE MUM.

Using stimulants, artificial devices and the support
of my carer, I'll bring bliss to female parts, draped in darkness.
My name will be enrolled in the Guinness Book of Records.

I want to be ushered into the Poetry Library,
where poems come dropping slow,
to sit with Neruda, Ritsos and Mayakovsky

and dream of the Nobel poet I could have been
had I not spent hours letting a librarian compose
erotic sonnets on my body with a quill.

Recharged, I will bungee-jump from Big Ben into the arms
of police. An international campaign of marches
and occupations will secure my release.

With a full TUC escort I'll be driven in an open top car
to Hyde Park and awarded the Labour Medal of Honour
for exemplary resistance to the State.

When my heart no longer pounds I'll be whisked
to the Organ Removal Unit where my parts
will be distributed to ailing poets.

I will make my ascension to Heaven, snuggle up to
Marilyn Monroe, and watch my state funeral below.
A day of world mourning will be declared.

Handkerchiefs will drop from the sky.

Dear NHS

I want all my bodily organs snipped,
placed on ice in a box, then strapped to a moped,
rushed to a helicopter pad and dropped
to their new owners in Falcarragh, Tijuana
and Havana and my blood syphoned into struggling sonneteers.

My heart, liver and eyes are to be forwarded
to a lyric tenor, a revolutionary peasant,
and a salsa instructor. Once they are fitted
and the settling-in period is done, a weekend
of toasting will commence with potteen, tequila, and rum.

What's left on the operating table
I bequeath to the skin and limb graft unit,
the hair transplant centre and the surgeons
who'll assemble with scalpels to peer and gasp
at my lower half, marvel at the god I must have been.

Notes

Dreep: to lower oneself from a height and drop the remaining distance.

Close: entrance to a tenement building.

Haun: hand.

Skite: to move quickly.

McAlpine's Fusiliers: a ballad regarded as the anthem of Irish construction workers in Britain.

Keek: a peek.

Squinching: to screw up the eyes or face.

Albert Einstein's essay 'Why Socialism?' was published in the first issue of the journal *Monthly Review* in May 1949 .

Sean-nos: ('old style') is a highly ornamented style of unaccompanied traditional Irish singing.

Pioneer pin: a lapel pin which alerts people not to offer alcohol or cigarettes to the wearer.

Acknowledgements

Thanks are due to the editors of the following publications, where some of these poems first appeared, sometimes in slightly different versions: *Acumen, The Bogmans Cannon, Cordite Poetry Review* (Australia), *Culture Matters, Cyphers, Dream Catcher, Galway Review, Glasgow Review of Books, Interpreter's House, Irish Left Review, Leitrim Observer, Live Encounters, London Grip, Magma, Militant Thistles, Mistress Quickly's Bed, Morning Star, New Welsh Review, North West Words, Poetry Ireland Review, Poetry Scotland, Poetry Salzburg Review* (Austria), *Red Poets, South Bank Poetry, Stand Magazine, Smoke, The North, The Poets Republic, The SHOp* and *The Yellow Nib*. Also the editors of following anthologies: Oliver Brennan, Todd Swift and Dominic Bury (eds) *The Poet's Quest for God* (2016), Mike Quille (ed), *On Fighting On!* (2017), Isabelle Kenyon (ed) *Please Hear What I'm Not Saying* (2018), Mike Quille (ed) *We Will Be Free!* (2018) and Matt Barnard (ed) *Poems for the NHS* (2018).

Special thanks go to Louise Nicholas, Caroline Maldonado, and the Pitshanger Poets who helped to steer these poems out of the shipyard.